The Garden Room

A play

Don Roberts

GU00724781

Samuel French—London
New York-Toronto-Hollywood

© 1992 BY SAMUEL FRENCH LTD

Rights of Performance by Amateurs are controlled by Samuel French Ltd, 52 Fitzroy Street, London W1P 6JR, and they, or their authorized agents, issue licences to amateurs on payment of a fee. **It is an infringement of the Copyright to give any performance or public reading of the play before the fee has been paid and the licence issued.**

The Royalty Fee indicated below is subject to contract and subject to variation at the sole discretion of Samuel French Ltd.

> Basic fee for each and every
> performance by amateurs   Code D
> in the British Isles

The publication of this play does not imply that it is necessarily available for performance by amateurs or professionals, either in the British Isles or Overseas. Amateurs and professionals considering a production are strongly advised in their own interests to apply to the appropriate agents for consent before starting rehearsals or booking a theatre or hall.

ISBN 0 573 03383 8

Please see page iv for further copyright information

Printed by
E. & E. PLUMRIDGE LTD., LINTON, CAMBRIDGE, ENGLAND

CHARACTERS

Lauretta Halton The eldest Halton sister
Constantia Phelps The second Halton sister
Clare Halton The third Halton sister
Susanna Morris The youngest Halton sister, aged between
    twenty-five and thirty-five

The action takes place in the conservatory of a neglected
Victorian house in the country

Time — Yesterday

COPYRIGHT INFORMATION
(See also page ii)

This play is fully protected under the Copyright Laws of the British Commonwealth of Nations, the United States of America and all countries of the Berne and Universal Copyright Conventions.

All rights, including Stage, Motion Picture, Radio, Television, Public Reading, and Translation into Foreign Languages, are strictly reserved.

No part of this publication may lawfully be reproduced in ANY form or by any means — photocopying, typescript, recording (including video-recording), manuscript, electronic, mechanical, or otherwise — or be transmitted or stored in a retrieval system, without prior permission.

Rights of Performance by Amateurs are controlled by Samuel French Ltd, 52 Fitzroy Street, London W1P 6JR, and they, or their authorized agents, issue licences to amateurs on payment of a fee. **It is an infringement of the Copyright to give any performance or public reading of the play before the fee has been paid and the licence issued.**

Licences are issued subject to the understanding that it shall be made clear in all advertising matter that the audience will witness an amateur performance; that the names of the authors of the plays shall be included on all announcements and on all programmes; and that the integrity of the authors' work will be preserved.

The Royalty Fee is subject to contract and subject to variation at the sole discretion of Samuel French Ltd.

In Theatres or Halls seatingFourHundred or more the fee will be subject to negotiation.

In Territories Overseas the fee quoted in this Acting Edition may not apply. A fee will be quoted on application to our local authorized agent, or if there is no such agent, on application to Samuel French Ltd, London.

VIDEO RECORDING OF AMATEUR PRODUCTIONS

Please note that the copyright laws governing video-recording are extremely complex and that it should not be assumed that any play may be video-recorded for *whatever purpose* without first obtaining the permission of the appropriate agents. The fact that a play is published by Samuel French Ltd does not indicate that video rights are available or that Samuel French Ltd controls such rights.

To the St. Anne's Afternoon Guild of Lytham St. Anne's, and to adventurous actresses in Townswomen's Guilds and Womens' Institutes anywhere.

THE GARDEN ROOM

A dilapidated conservatory. Night

The dilapidated conservatory acts as a corridor alongside a Victorian house. There is an exit R to the garden room and an exit L to the main part of the house. On the side of the conservatory towards the audience is an expanse of windows which is implied by lighting

There is a kitchen chair at a tatty little table with a table lamp. A few pots contain flowering plants. There are a couple of trays of seedlings. There is a glass of lemon cordial and a notebook open on the table with a pencil

As the CURTAIN *rises Clare is crocheting. She is dressed in slacks pulled over night attire. Occasionally she makes marks in the notebook. Sometimes she pauses in her work, listens intently and then returns to her work*

Then she hears the sound of someone walking deliberately quietly. She pauses in her work and waits expectantly to be interrupted

Constantia, wearing pyjamas with a touch of smartness when they were new, and a dressing-gown, enters from L and stops suddenly, surprised to see Clare

Constantia Clare! (*Defensively*) You can't work by that light!

Clare A better light than you think.
Constantia You'll strain your eyes.
Clare An easy stitch. Do it blindfold.

Clare sips the cordial

Constantia I didn't expect to find you here.
Clare Often sit here . Especially at night, when I'm wakeful
and got a pattern to finish for a magazine. You know I don't
need much sleep.
Constantia As far as I'm concerned it's a draughty corridor.
I'd find a better place to work. You could work in bed.
Clare I prefer sitting up.
Constantia You always want to be hard on yourself.
Clare Constantia, why are you up?
Constantia Couldn't sleep. Decided to stretch my legs.
There's room.
Clare You've always said you slept easily!
Constantia Perhaps it's because we have somebody new in
the house. You know how I sense things.
Clare Only our sister. Susanna has a right to be here. Good
that all four of us are together under one roof for the first
time for years.
Constantia I can't think of her as a sister. Hardly know her.
Odd days here, months, years away.

Constantia begins to pace irritably

Clare You must remember her. She's one of us. A Halton
through and through.
Constantia I was closest to Lauretta. Then to you.
Clare That's because Susanna married first.
Constantia She ran away.
Clare You always believed that.

Constantia Why has she come back this time?

Clare To rest. Recover. It's natural she should come here.

Constantia Without warning.

Clare There was no time.

Constantia You always favoured her. Rescuing lame ducks has always been a thing with you.

Clare Susanna has had a terrible journey.

Constantia She has hardly spoken to me.

Clare You've been out most of the time. She has talked to Lauretta. Always her more than either of us.

Constantia They looked through windows and deplored the garden.

Clare You must give Susanna time. Getting used to familiar things.

A strangled moan is heard from the garden room

Constantia Is that going on night after night?

Clare Most people make noise when they're asleep.

Constantia None of us do. Not like that. I've always slept soundly. She woke me several times last night. Even when I was asleep I was aware of her.

Clare She's been away a long time and I'm glad she's back.

Constantia Why are we beating around the bush? There is something the matter with Susanna. She shouldn't be here. The noises she makes.

Clare Days of travelling. Utterly washed out.

Constantia She's talked to you, of course!

Clare Briefly. Too briefly. About the heat on the journey. Going without food.

Constantia Why did she go there in the first place? She went with someone. She's not one for being on her own.

Clare She made the journey home on her own. Told Lauretta

there were strangers who joined her on the way and they
helped one another.

Another moan is heard from the garden room, softer this time

Constantia I suppose we should be thankful she escaped with
  her life. It's typical that she should have risked it in the first
  place.
Clare She couldn't have foreseen otherwise.
Constantia When we heard where she was, I told you it was a
  half savage place. If only you bothered to read the paper.
Clare I know you read it cover to cover. I've always wanted
  to be busy doing useful things.
Constantia Like mother. She acted the role of Lady Bounti-
  ful all her life, even when her stockings had holes in.
  Getting a power of attorney saved us and kept a roof over
  our heads.
Clare I know about your prescience. That's the word, isn't it.
  You've reminded us before.

Clare returns to her crochet work and her notebook

Constantia You might at least be grateful.
Clare Can't you be still! Do you need to pace up and down?

Constantia stops and turns aggressively

Constantia Or try to seem grateful.
Clare I've sometimes wondered whether a roof over our
  heads has become a millstone round our necks.
Constantia It's our home!
Clare A home is where you make it!

There is a sudden scream from the garden room. Constantia's whole body goes taut. But Clare hesitates for a moment and then continues her work

Constantia She shouldn't be here. In hospital!
Clare She has as much right as any of us.

Clare puts down her work, and moves towards the wings, listening intently. Then comes back on tiptoe

Clare Her door's ajar. I can hear her breathing. See her asleep through the crack in the opening. Only a nightmare! She was always prone to dreams and nightmares.
Constantia I don't remember. Anyway my room was upstairs.
Clare She always liked the garden room.

Clare resumes her seat and takes up her work

Constantia She did nothing to save the house.
Clare She was away. And anyway it's a mockery of what it was! The garden is dilapidated. Part of the front is shored up.
Constantia The insurance will pay for that.
Clare Have you ever asked yourself why she went away?
Constantia Because she wanted things all her own way. Quite selfish.
Clare Because she couldn't breathe here. And we all thwarted her.
Constantia She was as free as the rest of us.
Clare Her ideas were different. Mother wanted us all to be sensible. Art schools weren't.

Another moan is heard from the garden room

Constantia She goes on and on. We must talk to her. Make her see reason. She's home now for once!

Footsteps are heard. They wait for the appearance of Lauretta

Constantia Now the whole house is awake. It only wants the cats!

Clare They aren't interested in what we do. Except when we feed them or want their favourite chair for ourselves.

Lauretta enters L in a dressing-gown and night-dress. She is carrying a little tray with a mug .

Clare pauses in her work

Lauretta I hadn't realized you were both up until I saw the light.

Constantia What's that?

Lauretta Hot milk with a dash of something. It's always helped Susanna sleep in the old days. I'd been listening to her. Decided it was time.

Clare That's good of you. I think she's still asleep.

Constantia And it's not the old days. She should be in hospital where she can be properly cared for.

Lauretta This is the best place. Where she's loved.

Constantia As if she'd notice.

Lauretta You're being unkind about Susanna. She's our flesh and blood.

Constantia Looking the facts in the face.

Lauretta We can help her better than anyone else.

Constantia She'll take as much help as you can give and then some more. Start sucking blood.

Clare I hope you never want help, Constantia.
Constantia I'm not likely to. I'll see to that.
Lauretta We all do, sooner or later.

A stifled moan is heard from the garden room

Lauretta I'll take Susanna her drink before it gets cold.
Constantia She's moaning in her sleep again.
Lauretta Susanna won't mind being wakened for a drink.
Constantia It's ridiculous. Don't you know it's the middle of
    the night?
Lauretta A little after four.
Constantia Leave her alone. (*She bars Lauretta's way*)
    She's already woken us all. No knowing what she'll do or
    say when she's disturbed. We'll never get to sleep.
Lauretta Please let me by.
Constantia No point.
Clare Lauretta knows what she's doing.
Constantia I can't believe either of you do. Or think.
Lauretta If you knock me I shall drop it. And that will
    frighten her. She's been frightened enough. You've only
    got to look at her.

*Constantia seems deterred by the remark and eventually steps
aside*

Constantia Very well then. It's on your head.

Lauretta continues on her way and exits

*She is watched in their different ways by her sisters. Clare
moistens her lips and then resumes her work*

Clare I think you forget Lauretta is a district nurse.

Constantia Part time! Have you realized what it means if Susanna stays?

Clare We all have equal shares in the house.

Constantia We've never seen a penny towards the upkeep.

Clare She always helped with the garden.

Constantia Last time she was here was three years ago.

Clare You were away. She worked like a trooper.

Constantia I've got the lad from Yardley's farm coming next week in the evening to help with the heavy work.

Clare I didn't know that. I almost put a notice in the post office.

Constantia Arranged it when I was at Yardley's doing their books yesterday. He's a strapping lad and bright. Knows what needs to be done without having to be watched.

Clare You might have said.

Constantia You were both so intent on Susanna I had no chance. And that's another thing. We'll have to keep her away from him.

Clare What are you suggesting? (*She pauses in her work*)

Constantia You know very well.

Clare I do not.

Constantia Clare! You can't be that green. Don't pretend.

Clare That was years ago.

Constantia For that and other reasons we must get her away. She'd be better cared for somewhere else. Here there will always be questions.

Clare She has her rights here. (*Her voice rising*) And that was always her room.

Constantia Keep your voice down. Lauretta is quite likely to have left the door open. We know how thoughtless she is.

Clare It's you who destroy our quiet.

Clare puts her work on the table and rises to look out of the window of the conservatory — towards the audience.

Constantia sighs but her manner changes

Constantia I see I'm expected to bend! Very well! I know
how much you love the garden. You'll be pleased to see it
looking in better order. Joey's a hard worker.

Clare You should have married again.

Constantia Once was enough!

Clare You'd have preferred a place of your own.

Constantia I came back to save the house.

Clare Yes, you always felt for it, loved it. Susanna suffo-
cated here and went away. You came back because you
can't let go. I should have stayed away. Only Lauretta
really belongs here.

Constantia What nonsense you're talking! I thought we'd
start Joey clearing against the wall over there and work
backwards towards us.

Clare It's definite he's coming?

Constantia Quite definite. He'll earn some pin money and
get a supper, and we'll start to see order in the wilderness.

Clare I have to agree it's been worrying me. I know Joey by
sight. He'll be a help.

Constantia One thing less to worry about then!

*Steps are heard. Constantia moves away from the window and
Clare slows the pace of her work*

Constantia What's that you're making?

Clare An evening shawl. Eventually. It's what the magazine
ordered.

Constantia Fancy you designing an evening shawl! You
never go out in the evenings to anywhere where they'd wear
a shawl.

Clare I can imagine I do.

Lauretta is heard approaching

They watch for her. She enters from the garden room without the glass and tray

Lauretta I didn't have to wake her. She was half awake. Dozing. She was glad of the drink.

Constantia Making terrible noises. Doesn't she know how disturbing they are!

Lauretta She doesn't know.

Constantia Then she ought to.

Lauretta Don't you think there is something we ought to do! Think of her more kindly. We have no idea what she has gone through in the last six weeks. Perhaps we can guess from the newspapers and the television. Let things be. I don't mind getting up in the night to bring her a drink. It's not much. Clare hasn't minded sitting there just in case.

Constantia So the whole house is to be disordered just for her.

Lauretta It is only you who are making a fuss.

Constantia She should go somewhere where they can care for her. If that is the trouble! Or is it the usual of just sucking up as much sympathy as possible and getting it by every means she knows?

Lauretta Not, I think this time!

Constantia So you admit it has been.

Lauretta I always think when somebody is craving sympathy, they're ill. Perhaps not in the way they say. But they need something.

Constantia You're a soft touch, Lauretta.

Clare Do you always have to be picking quarrels, Constantia?

Constantia Why do you two never want to see?
Clare There's no need for us all to sit up.
Lauretta I'll take your place at the table and you can both go
   to bed. If Susanna wakes I'll be here. She's come back to
   us because she wants to rest and be quiet. There was
   nowhere else she could go.
Constantia So she remembered us for once!

*Susanna, looking drawn and dressed in a woollen gown, has
come in unobserved from the garden room. Her hair shows
signs of having been cared for and dyed but is now a ruin*

Susanna Yes. (*She looks from one to another*) Yes.

*They stare at her, feeling that such a simple word doesn't convey
anything. Clare rises and goes towards her*

Clare Take my chair.
Susanna I'd rather stand for a moment and look into the
   garden.

She stands facing the garden (the audience)

Clare Nothing much to see yet, is there?
Susanna The sun is beginning to show. I can see everything.
   Albertine disporting all over the wall. I'm glad nobody's
   cut her back. The hollyhocks — they've just finished. I like
   to see them with all their seed pods. But I'd hoped to catch
   them in flower.
Clare It's still too dark for me to see properly.
Susanna Not for me, Clare. Over a week ago the dark was
   closing in on me and I remembered my garden room and
   this scene constantly. I'd fix my mind on it as the end of my

journey. I'd stumble along in the cold of the desert night
and see the garden just out of touch before me. Yesterday
morning I walked in the garden when you and Constantia
were still asleep. I drank in the scent of those old fashioned
pinks. Lauretta brought me a drink and we sat and talked.

Lauretta The dew soaked us through. Had to change.

Susanna I went back to bed, Lauretta tucked me in and I
slept like a child. I didn't even dream of gardens.

Lauretta You're safe here, Susanna.

Susanna I don't think I'll ever feel safe again. Even here.

Lauretta Out there in the garden among your favourite
flowers.

Susanna Until you came, I stood against the laurels feeling
frightened. I could walk no further. The garden was open to
anybody.

Constantia The gate's waiting to be mended.

*The light begins to change as if dawn is starting outside. Shafts
come into the room*

*Clare thinks it better to talk of ordinary things as if it would help
Susanna*

Clare Some time.

Constantia We shall have the insurance money soon. I've
got all the plans in my head, how to get the most of it.

Susanna I think I'd like to go into the garden.

Lauretta There's a bit of a wind and you'll get soaked from
the dew.

Susanna I must have air, Lauretta. I like the feel of dew.

Lauretta It isn't properly light yet.

Susanna I can see.

Lauretta Do you want me to come with you?

Susanna No! If you watch me from here, I'll feel safe. I'll turn round when I want to see you're watching. I'll keep in sight of this window.

Susanna moves slowly across the stage and off

The others exchange silent looks

Constantia She is impossible. Worse than ever. Things can't go on like this. Walking in a wet garden at this hour.

Lauretta None of us know what has happened to her, what has been done to her. Perhaps if it had happened to us, we'd be begging for sympathy.

Clare Whatever it was, I don't think I could have survived.

Lauretta There she is. Looking towards Albertine. It was always her favourite rose.

Constantia Rampages everywhere!

Clare She can't really see!

Lauretta How silly of me! The garden light still works. I put it on the other time.

Lauretta hurries off

Constantia I think she is enjoying all this upset.

Clare Lauretta likes being useful. And she knows how.

Constantia Clare, it's clear to me that only you and I can sort this business out.

Clare We must give Susanna time.

Constantia The longer it goes on, the worse she'll get. Nothing but indulging her. Won't help her one little bit in the long run.

Clare Try talking to her.

Constantia She's not rational. At dinner last night, glum. Didn't seem to respond to anything said to her. Must make some effort.

Clare Ask Lauretta what she knows. They were always close. I think perhaps she's gleaned more than she's admitting.

Constantia They only talked of the garden. Lauretta couldn't lie to save her life. It will all be up to you and me. The practical ones. You know that. We've sorted things out together before. And better the family than outsiders where Susanna is concerned! We don't want things talked about locally. We had to live several escapades down.

The light suddenly increases because Lauretta has turned on the garden light

Do you see that? We noticed the change in the light. Susanna didn't move an inch.Still staring at Albertine from over here.

Clare Always her favourite rose. She has to get used to things. Give her time.

Clare turns from looking out, takes a sip of her cordial and takes up her work again

Constantia How long? You keep saying "Give her time" or words to that effect, but you never say how long, how much time? Never make it clear when we should do something positive.

Clare We have to be patient.

Constantia That's you all over. Sit by the tidemarks and watch and wait. When you've decided the tide will be over us and it will be too late.

Clare I'll know when the time comes. There is no other way. Believe me, Constantia.

Constantia Believe you!

Clare Why is it that on practically every subject in the world
you are calm almost to the point of indifference? Except
Susanna who is your own flesh and blood. About her, you
are unkind, unfeeling, unhelpful.

Constantia (*shouting*) That is very unfair.

Clare There is no need to shout!

Constantia You sit there, rabbitting away with your shawl,
pretending to care. Observing. But doing absolutely
nothing positive to help.

Clare I asked you to stop shouting. Please!

Constantia Why is it that where she is concerned you are
impossible?

Clare pauses in her work and stares in disbelief

Clare I can hardly believe what you're saying.

Constantia You see what she does to us. Proves what I've
been saying. She can't stay.

Clare You have never liked her!

Constantia I have never liked the way she comes and goes as
it suits her, never liked the way her hands are always open
for help. I have never liked the way we have rescued her
time and again from scrapes and she never learns anything.

There is a cry off stage. Suddenly Clare is on her feet

Clare Lauretta has her arms round her. She's bringing her in
from the garden.

*Constantia does not respond. She purses her lips and stares out
into the garden, and then turns a little to watch for the entrance
of Lauretta and Susanna*

Clare You are to say nothing. Nothing!
Constantia I will do what seems appropriate.
Clare You don't know, I don't know what is appropriate!

Lauretta enters, holding Susanna protectively

Lauretta One of you please get something warm to put round
her. She is chilled to the bone.

For a moment nobody moves

Clare The old overcoat in the hall!

Clare hurries out

Lauretta rubs Susanna's hands

Constantia Best place would be in bed.
Susanna I want to be free to stand or sit.
Lauretta Here then! (*Lauretta guides Susanna to the chair
Clare has left vacant*)
Susanna I'm sorry, Lauretta. I couldn't face it outside any
longer. I know it's silly to be frightened of shadows and by
noises. Lots of little tiny noises. But I was frightened.
Lauretta It will pass.
Susanna I can't go on if it doesn't.
Constantia You need help.
Susanna I need to be here. That's why I came home. I need
to be here. I heard what you were saying when I was lying
in bed. I won't be sent away! You can't send me!

Constantia and Lauretta are stunned by the revelation

The discomfiture is reduced by the return of Clare. She is carrying a voluminous mannish overcoat which is very worn and faded

Clare Let me tuck it round you.
Susanna Thank you. Just on my shoulders. I know you
   mean to be kind.
Clare Slip it on.

Susanna rises almost mechanically and allows herself to be put in the coat

Lauretta You'll soon be warm.
Susanna Yes. But that's not where I'm chilled. Out there I
   heard the gate move in the wind and I realized it was wide
   open. Like the gate on the apartment block when I got back
   with the visas.
Lauretta You're safe here. We always keep the gate open.
   It's always left open to help the milkman, anyway.
Susanna It doesn't matter whether they're open or not.
   They'll always get in. I ran all the way to the apartment. I
   knew the door would be open.(*She stops and looks around
   her*)
Lauretta You don't need to go on.
Susanna I don't, do I. Out there in the garden, I decided I
   would talk. If I didn't, Constantia would send me away.
   And I'm not going.
Clare Constantia can't send you away. This is our home.
Susanna She always gets her own way. Her face is full of
   schemes. Your eyes are full of questions.
Lauretta Perhaps it's better if you talk.
Susanna Say what comes into my head! I can't do it any
   other way. I'm trying to be rational. Our apartment door

open, you could see it had been broken open. Selim – he was
my friend – was on the floor, pushed against the wall. Two
soldiers were searching him. One of them didn't look much
more than a boy. He clipped Selim's gold watch on his wrist.
They all looked at me. Then Selim shut his eyes. I wanted to
run, but somebody grabbed me from behind and held me. The
soldier who had taken the wristwatch cut Selim's throat—just
like that—and I thought 'He's done it before a thousand times'
and waited for him to cut mine. It was like a slow motion film
and I died.

Constantia That's enough! Like a slow motion film! You're
making it worse than it was! Take a hold of yourself!

*Clare goes to embrace Susanna, but Susanna draws back and
contact isn't made. Clare steps back, abashed*

Susanna Leave me alone! Don't anybody touch me!
Lauretta In your own time.
Susanna You want to know! (*She points at Constantia*) Even
she wants to know!
Constantia I'm not going to indulge your fantasies!
Susanna Not fantasies. I lived through it.
Lauretta I know that.
Susanna Why I came home!

*The light has increased as the sun rises, casting a pinkish glow on
the stage, but also leaving shafts of shadow*

Lauretta You don't have to tell us. If you want to, we'll
listen.
Susanna Some things aren't clear. I can't remember what I
felt. I can't remember if I felt anything.
Clare Gently.

Susanna They pushed me into the bedroom. The young one took me first then the other three. I closed my eyes and waited for them to cut my throat. I could hear jabbering, then banging, drawers thrown on the floor, felt the sun streaming in. Suddenly there were noises in the street, shouting and shooting. When I opened my eyes, I was alone.

She closes her eyes, stretching out her arms, and Lauretta holds her

I lay there waiting. After a while I knew they wouldn't be back. I snatched some clean clothes from the pile they'd scattered. I found the visas lying by the door. There was a rucksack and I stuffed some things in. I remembered a warm sweater and another pair of shoes. I also remembered Selim. I took a spare sheet, opened it out, and then with my eyes shut went into the lounge and put it over him. When I opened my eyes, I'd managed to cover most of him. I'd covered his head, that's what mattered. In the kitchen, everything was on the floor. They'd left me some packets of biscuits, a pack of dates, pistachio nuts and a bag of sugar lumps. I shoved them in the rucksack. I found a tin of condensed milk and I ate it with a spoon, scraped every bit of it. Didn't know when I'd eat next. I looked around, trying to be sensible. The only thing I could find was an eggplant and I ate that. The door of the apartment was still open. I could hear other doors banging, the wind had got up. I wanted to take one last look at Selim but didn't dare. We'd shared everything for the last six months, neither of us had cared for anybody so much before. But I crept out — I didn't want that memory of him — and along the corridor towards the light.

Susanna breaks away from Lauretta

In the courtyard was the body of the young soldier. There was a black hole in the middle of his face. Selim's watch had gone. I'd meant to walk slowly, but for the next three miles I ran and ran until I was outside the city. Nobody stopped me, people were hurrying in all directions. When it was dark I found another woman and a bandaged child sheltering against a burnt out tank. We huddled together and slept till dawn. We were all terrified and cold.

Lauretta Susanna, you've told us enough now. Be easy. We understand.

Susanna No-one will ever understand — there's more but my lips are dry.

Clare exchanges a look with Lauretta and leaves in the direction of the main part of the house

Lauretta Gently then. No need to talk for a while. Cry if you want to.

Susanna I've done all the crying I'll ever do.

Lauretta It helps.

Constantia Better to shut things out completely. From now, just forget everything. Blot it out – start afresh.

Lauretta It's not easy to do that.

Constantia Things like that don't happen here. Going over it only makes things worse. Tell her I'm right, Lauretta. Tell her to blot it all out. She does listen to you.

Susanna Don't talk about me as if I'm not here! I loved Selim. I can't, won't pretend he didn't happen. I don't want your pity, you never liked me! Don't want me back!

Lauretta Nothing has to be hurried. And you'll have all the time you need. You're safe here.

Susanna Safe. I'll never feel safe again. Anywhere. (*She looks hectically about*) I look out there into the garden. I know it's our garden. But the shadows are like burnt out vehicles, gaping holes, bodies. Over there, there's the shape of ... so many terrible shapes.

Clare enters with a glass of lime juice

Clare Moisten your lips with this.

Susanna drinks from the glass and gives it back

Susanna We begged water when we could. Like dirty water collected during the night in petrol cans. Licked it out of puddles. Walked for days. Some days there were only three or four of us. Some days there seemed to be hundreds. We all went in the same direction. Follow my leader. I just hoped it was the right way. When we heard aeroplanes, we lay down in the sand and it scorched us. At night I put on all my clothes to keep warm. We shared what food we had, I, the woman and the child. The bandages got dirtier and the child whimpered more and more. We walked, staggered for days. I even prayed.

Susanna stretches her hand out for the glass. Clare gives it to her and she drinks from it

Then early in the morning, when it was still dark, I heard whirring sounds nearby. When the sun came up, there were tanks and men watching us. I heard orders and some of them came towards us, you couldn't see their eyes. Their faces were covered with goggles, and their guns were pointed at us. I no longer cared, as long as they killed us quickly. Then I heard our language. Minutes later we were being fed and a young soldier squeezed orange juice for the child. We were saved. They put us in a lorry and drove us away so fast it hurt. I began to cry.

Hours later the soldiers put me in a tent and I cried for two days. I even cried as I ate. Nobody seemed to mind.

Lauretta We won't mind. Now we will understand. So glad to have you safe home.

Susanna Safe! What does that matter. Selim is lying out there in his blood.

Susanna rushes off stage

After a moment of exchanged glances, Lauretta follows her

A prolonged scream and sobbing is heard. Constàntia seems even more on edge, resentful, even disturbed, but Clare looks with calm concern into the garden. When the dialogue is resumed, the screaming and sobbing begins to subside but continues as a sound until the end of the play

Clare Now it will be easier for her.

Constantia Easier? After that display! She's feeding on it. Are we to have that night after night! Look at them. So touching! Lauretta is being imposed on.

Clare She is very patient and understanding. She knows instinctively when to hold Susanna. I couldn't do that. I haven't the warmth.

Constantia I will ring for the doctor. He'll take Susanna where she can be treated properly. Break the cycle. We can't cope.

Clare You will do no such thing!

Constantia I most certainly will.

Clare You will do no such thing. Susanna stays here. She knew what she wanted when she came here. She wants love and our care. Lauretta and I decided to give it. She knows now that she will have it. And you, Constantia will stay and

cope. Think about giving love. You're not running away
from giving for once. She's our flesh and blood!

*For a moment it looks as though Constantia will not be deterred,
but then she confronts what is being said as she faces Clare's
unwavering look. Constantia subsides into a chair, totally
subordinate to Clare. She begins to cry*

CURTAIN

FURNITURE AND PROPERTY LIST

On stage :   Tatty little table. *On it* : glass of lemon cordial,
                note book, pencil, crochet work
           Few earthenware pots containing flowering
                plants
           Couple of trays of seedlings
           Kitchen chair

Off stage :   Little tray (**Lauretta**)
           Mug (**Lauretta**)
           Man's faded and worn overcoat (**Lauretta**)
           Glass of lime juice (**Clare**)

LIGHTING PLOT

Practical fitting required: table lamp
Interior. The same throughout

To open :   Practical on with covering spot

Cue 1   **Constantia:"**... waiting to be mended"   (Page 12)
              Dawn breaking effect, gradually increasing

Cue 2   **Constantia** "several escapades down"   (Page 13)
              Short pause: snap on light effect from garden

Cue 3   **Susanna:** "Why I came home!"   (Page 18)
              *Increase dawn effect to pinkish glow with shafts
                 of shadow*